Written by **JANET HALFMANN**   Illustrated by **DARLA OKADA**

How can we be kind?

WISDOM FROM THE ANIMAL KINGDOM

Inspiring | Educating | Creating | Entertaining

Brimming with creative inspiration, how-to projects, and useful information to enrich your everyday life, Quarto is a favorite destination for those pursuing their interests and passions.

First published in the US in 2022 by Frances Lincoln Children's, an imprint of The Quarto Group.
100 Cummings Center, Suite 265D, Beverly, MA 01915, USA.
T +1 978-282-9590 F +1 078 -283-2742 www.Quarto.com

A CIP record for this book is available from the Library of Congress.

ISBN 978-0-7112-6879-1
eISBN 978-0-7112-6881-4

The illustrations were created digitally.
Set in New Spirit

Published by Katie Cotton & Peter Marley
Designed by Myrto Dimitrakoulia
Edited by Hattie Grylls
Production by Dawn Cameron

Manufactured in Guangdong, China TT032022
1 3 5 7 9 8 6 4 2

How can we be kind?

How can we

be kind?

We can look
after each other,
like **European
badgers** do.

We can make
everyone feel welcome,

like **capybaras** do.

And we can share
with others,
like **jackdaws** do.

How can we
be kind?

We can work as a team,
like **ants** and **bees** do.

We can wait for others,

like **African elephants** do.

We can put others first,
like **prairie dogs** do.

And we can make
others laugh,
like **orangutans** do.

How can we be kind?

We can help others shine,

like **blue manakins** do.

We can eat together,

like **white pelicans** do.

And we can include everyone,

like father
emus do.

How can we be kind?

We can stick up
for our friends,
like **zebras** do.

We can look

after our families,

like **banded mongooses** do.

We can help others
on their way,

like **dolphins** do.

And we can comfort
those who are upset,

like
chimpanzees do.

How will you

be kind?

Meet the Animals

European Badgers

European badgers live in clans that usually include six to eight animals. They like to dig their tunnel homes, called setts, in woodlands. Fleas and lice live and feed on badgers, so clan mates clean each other's fur. The helpers tackle hard-to-reach places, keeping the entire clan healthy.

Capybaras

Capybaras live in small groups near water in Central and South America. They are super friendly and very chatty—purring, clicking, whistling, and more. All kinds of animals—birds, turtles, monkeys, and ducks—like to sit atop these large rodents while they graze on water plants or wallow in the mud.

Jackdaws

Jackdaws are in the crow family. They live in Europe, western Asia, and North Africa. These noisy birds are smart and very social. Young jackdaws share their favorite foods with their friends. They are even more generous than primates like the chimpanzee. Jackdaws eat many foods, but mostly seeds, insects, and fruit.

Ants and Bees

Ants and bees live in large colonies. Everyone in the group works together for the good of all. The queen lays all of the eggs. The rest of the colony is made up of some males and mostly workers, who are all female. The workers take care of the queen and the babies, search for food, and build and protect the nest.

African Elephants

African female elephants and their calves live in a group, called a herd. They live mainly in Africa's grasslands and rainforests. The herd will stop if one of them falls behind. A group member might be slow because of an injured leg. The herd wants to wait for her, because she will struggle to protect herself if she gets separated from the rest.

Prairie Dogs

Prairie dogs are found in North American grasslands. They live in family groups called coteries within large underground towns. They take turns standing guard. *Chirk-chirk-chirk!* A guard spots a hawk. The prairie dog's warning attracts attention to himself, putting him in more danger. He signals anyway, so the others can be safe.

Orangutans

Orangutans live in the rainforests of the Southeast Asian islands of Sumatra and Borneo. These great apes spend most of their lives in the trees and mostly eat fruit. Young orangutans like to play. They make play faces and laugh as they wrestle. Their playmates often can't help chuckling right along with them!

Blue Manakins

In the forests of South America, blue manakin male birds gather to sing and dance for females. Only the main male in the group mates, and the others make him look good. One after another, a chorus line of male birds tweet, leap, and flutter before the female. The show ends with a solo dance by the main male—and hopefully the female's approval!

White Pelicans

The white pelicans of North America hunt fish while swimming on the surface of the water. They are known for working together. A flock of birds will line up and surround the fish. Once the fish are trapped, the birds scoop them up with their huge pouched bills—and everyone gets a meal!

Emus

Emus are the second-largest birds in the world, found only in Australia. The emu father is a great parent! He sits on up to fifteen eggs for eight weeks. When the chicks hatch, he leads them from the nest to find food and water. If he comes upon lost chicks from other broods, he includes them in his big family. The father emu teaches and protects the chicks for up to two years.

Zebras

Zebras are found in the grasslands of southern Africa. They graze in family groups that are part of a large herd. Lions or hyenas try to separate a single zebra from the group to capture it more easily. But hungry predators can expect a fight. *RUMBLE-RUMBLE-RUMBLE!* Herd members thunder to the aid of the animal in trouble, driving off the attackers.

Banded Mongooses

Banded mongooses are from southern Africa. They live in groups called packs. The entire pack raises the babies, called pups. At first, some members stay behind to babysit the newborns while the pack hunts termites and beetles. When the pups are old enough to go along, pack members help to protect them. What a caring family!

Dolphins

Dolphins travel in pods ranging from two to forty animals. They are well known for helping out their own and other animals. In Canada, dolphins helped a young seal that had swum into shallow water. The seal couldn't get back to sea because of the strong current, so the dolphins nudged the little one along.

Chimpanzees

Chimpanzees live in small groups within large communities. When these great apes get hurt in a leopard attack or are upset, comfort is nearby. Group mates lick and clean the wounds of the injured. They shower those who are suffering with kisses and hugs. Infants and young chimpanzees are the biggest comforters of all!